Holt Spanish 2

Standardized Assessment Tutor

Printed in the United States of America

ISBN 0-03-074557-8
1 2 3 4 5 6 7   170   06 05 04

Table of Contents

SPANISH LEVEL 2

To the Teacher

Teachers in all disciplines are being called upon to help prepare students to take standardized reading, writing, and math tests. As a language teacher, you are already targeting many of the same skills that your students will need in order to perform well on standardized tests. Using the *¡Exprésate! Standardized Assessment Tutor*, your students can continue to practice these skills while learning Spanish.

The practice tests in this book are presented in a format similar to that of many state-approved standardized tests. If your students are familiar with the test formats, they may experience lower levels of anxiety and therefore perform better when faced with an actual test. Because the content of the practice tests is closely tied to what your students are learning in class, they will remain focused on your course objectives as they prepare to be tested in other disciplines.

The *¡Exprésate! Standardized Assessment Tutor* also includes strategies for taking reading, writing, and math tests. Before you give each practice test, you may want to remind students to use specific strategies.

Reading Tests

Each chapter contains three practice reading tests. Your students will read a variety of selections, including narratives, letters, and realia. Each reading passage is followed by a series of multiple-choice questions that ask students to perform the kinds of tasks they will perform when taking standardized reading tests, such as identifying facts and details, inferring information, skimming and scanning, making predictions, and finding main ideas. At the same time, your students will be given the opportunity to apply the reading strategies they have been learning in your language class. The following is an excerpt from one of the practice reading tests.

A Read the following article that Mariana has written for her school newspaper. Then, choose the correct ending for each statement that follows.

> Cada año celebramos la Nochevieja, el último día del año. Nos reunimos con toda nuestra familia, pensamos en el año que va y en el año que viene y nos divertimos mucho.

1 The **Nochevieja** is celebrated on
  A December 24.
  B July 4.
  C December 31.
  D September 16.   (correct answer: December 31)

Writing Tests

The practice writing tests target several of the written composition objectives articulated for standardized writing tests in English. In addition to writing letters and dialogues, your students will have an opportunity to develop their narrative, expository, and persuasive skills. Here is an example taken from one of the practice writing tests.

Narrative writing Imagine that you recently gave a party for Mother's or Father's Day. Write an e-mail in Spanish to a friend, describing what you did to prepare for it. Then, describe three things everyone did at the party. Finally, say how the party went.

Math Tests

Each level of the *¡Exprésate! Standardized Assessment Tutor* includes two practice math tests that target math concepts related to the cultural topics your students will learn in class, such as using the metric system to measure height, weight, and distance, and using illustrations and graphs to perform tasks like currency and temperature conversions. As your students practice math, they will further develop their ability to function within a Spanish-speaking society. The following is an example from one of the practice math tests.

The temperatures on the chart below are given in degrees Celsius. Use the formula $T_F = \frac{9}{5} T_C + 32$ to convert temperatures from Celsius to Fahrenheit.

(T_F = temperature in Fahrenheit; T_C = temperature in Celsius) Round to the nearest degree.

ESPAÑA: Pronóstico para el 18 de marzo

Ciudad	hoy mínimo/máximo °C	mañana mínimo/máximo °C
La Coruña	15/19	15/17
Barcelona	14/20	13/25
Córdoba	9/24	9/25
Madrid	12/17	11/19
Málaga	10/23	11/26
Sevilla	11/24	10/25
Valencia	17/21	17/23

1 ¿Cuál va a ser la temperatura máxima para mañana en Málaga?

  A 26° F

  B 52° F

  C 73° F

  D 79° F   (correct answer: D)

To the Student: Test-taking Strategies

If you are among the many students who would like to do well on standardized tests, you may want to practice some test-taking strategies. The suggestions below can help you feel more confident and perform better on standardized reading, writing, and math tests.

General Test-taking Strategies

Read directions carefully.

Make sure you understand what you're supposed to do in each section of a test. If you're not sure, ask for clarification. Don't try to guess what the directions mean and don't make assumptions.

Don't spend too much time on one question.

If you don't know the answer to a question, don't waste valuable time on it. Move on to the next question. When answering a series of questions about a single topic, a later question may provide a clue. Mark any questions you skip so you don't forget to come back to them.

Use the process of elimination.

Use the process of elimination. Read all of the choices before marking your answer. Eliminate those that are obviously incorrect, then choose the best answer from the remaining choices.

Use all of the time available.

If you finish a test and you still have some time left, check your work. Check your answers again and proofread. Use any extra time to eliminate careless mistakes.

Be prepared.

Nothing builds your test-taking confidence like knowing that you're prepared. As you study, mentally quiz yourself by asking yourself questions. If you don't readily know the answers, study some more!

Be informed.

Find out about the test beforehand. Ask your teacher what you'll need to know and what kinds of questions you'll be asked. Taking practice tests can help you prepare for the actual test. Being familiar with the format of a test can help you feel more at ease.

Strategies for Reading Tests

The main goal of the reading sections of standardized tests is to determine your understanding of the reading passage. Questions may focus on the main idea, or they may check your understanding of the details of the passage. A correct answer may be stated clearly in the text, or you may have to make inferences and draw conclusions based on information provided.

Look at the big picture.

Examine the most obvious features of the text. Decide what type of reading selection it is. Is it an article, a letter, or perhaps an advertisement? What do the pictures or illustrations tell you? Look for information in the titles and headings.

Read the entire passage before answering questions.

Skim the selection to get a general overview of the topic and the tone of the passage. If you do not understand at first, keep reading. At this point, focus on understanding the main idea of the passage. Consider details later.

Read the questions.

Read all of the questions so you'll know what information to look for when you reread the passage. Don't read the answer choices and don't mark any answers yet.

Reread the passage.

Once you have a general idea of what the passage is about and you know what the questions are, read the passage a second time. As you reread, underline any information that relates to the questions.

Answer the questions in your own words.

Try to answer each question in your mind before considering the answer choices, then look for a similar answer among the choices provided. Be sure to read all of the answer choices and mark the best one.

When in doubt, read again.

If the answer you expected is not among your choices, reread the passage. Look especially at any sections you underlined. Check for any words you may have misunderstood. Use context clues to help you figure out what any unfamiliar words mean.

Make your best guess.

If you've completed the steps above and you're still not sure, mark the answer that seems most likely to be correct. Ask your teacher if you should answer every question or if you are penalized for guessing incorrectly.

Strategies for Writing Tests

The main goal of a writing test is to determine your ability to express yourself clearly in writing. Clear writing is well-organized and free of grammatical and spelling errors.

Determine the purpose of your writing.

You may be asked to write for a variety of purposes. For example, writing assignments may require you to describe something, to tell a story, or to support an opinion. Decide what the purpose of each assignment is and remain focused on that purpose as you write.

Create a brief outline.

Before you begin writing, gather your thoughts. Briefly outline the main points you want to include and put your ideas in order. List any vocabulary words you'll want to use.

Write a topic statement.

Write a single sentence that clearly states the main idea of your writing. You may or may not include this sentence in your finished assignment. Its purpose is to keep you focused on the writing task.

Think of a title.

Like a topic statement, a title can keep you focused on your writing purpose, even if you revise it later or eliminate it completely from your finished product.

Write thoughtfully and completely.

Follow directions completely and make sure your writing assignment is complete. If you have time, double-check by rereading directions after you've finished writing. Remember, most types of writing should have an introduction, a body, and a conclusion. Letters should contain a greeting and a closing.

Use your imagination.

When creating a story or other type of writing for a test, try writing from the point of view of someone else. Using your imagination is fun and it can save you valuable time during a test.

Read it.

When you've finished writing, read what you've written. Make sure it makes sense and flows well. Add any details you may have left out.

Proofread it.

Reread your work to check for grammar and spelling errors. If you have time, you may want to read it several times, looking for a different type of error each time.

Strategies for Math Tests

The purpose of a math test is to determine your ability to perform mathematical functions such as addition, subtraction, multiplication, and division, to solve equations.

List the given and unknown values.

You may be asked to solve word-problems or derive information from graphs or charts. Some of the information you'll need to solve the problem will be provided. First, list the information that is provided (the given values), and then what information is missing (the unknown values).

Given values: value of 1 U.S. dollar = $1.50 Canadian currency

price of a book in Canadian dollars = $16.50

Unknown value: price of the book in U.S. dollars = ?

Write out the equation.

Math problems must be converted into equations in order to be solved. To calculate the price of the book in U.S. currency, you'd need to solve the following equation.

price of book ÷ value of 1 U.S. dollar = price of book in U.S. dollars

Insert the known values into the equation.

Once you know what the equation is, you can plug in the information you need to solve it. For the currency conversion described above, the equation is as follows:

$16.50 ÷ $1.50 = _____

Solve the equation.

To solve the equation, perform the necessary multiplication, division, addition, or subtraction as needed. Remember to show your work if required.

$16.50 ÷ $1.50 = $11.00

Recheck your answer.

Whenever possible, recheck your work by working the problem in a different way. For example, to check your division, multiply the divisor ($1.50) by your answer ($11.00). The result should be the dividend ($16.50).

original problem: $16.50 ÷ 1.50 = 11.00$ recheck: $11.00 \times 1.50 = 16.50$

Evaluate your solution.

Make sure your solution answers the question asked. Ask yourself whether or not your answer makes sense.

Overcoming Test Anxiety

Test-taking makes many people a little anxious, but you can use strategies to overcome your worries and perform better on tests.

Be well-prepared physically.

You should arrive at a test well-rested and well-fed. Get a good night's sleep and be sure to set your alarm. Lack of sleep and poor nutrition can hurt your ability to concentrate.

Talk to your teacher about your feelings.

If you're feeling anxious about a test, tell your teacher how you're feeling. Ask what you can do to feel better prepared. Your teacher knows your abilities well and is likely to give some personalized suggestions to help you.

Don't be distracted by other students.

Focus on your own performance on the test. Sit in a place where you won't be distracted by your classmates. Don't worry if others finish before you. A smart test-taker uses any extra time to recheck answers.

Avoid negative discussions with other students.

While studying with others is a good idea, do not indulge in discussions about how worried you are or how unfair your situation seems. Such talk is not helpful and it will only increase your anxiety.

Have a positive attitude.

As you begin to take a test, think positively. Remind yourself that you have studied well and that you are prepared. Negative thoughts can interfere with your performance, so push them right out of your head!

Relax.

As you wait for the test to begin, remind yourself of all the things you've done to prepare. Take a deep breath, relax, and do your best.

Holt Spanish 2

Practice Tests

Familiares y amigos

CAPÍTULO **1**

READING

A Read the following e-mail from Lorenzo to his new friend Alonso. Then choose the best answer for each question that follows.

Estimado Alonso,

Me gustaría mucho decirte cómo es mi vida aquí en Estados Unidos. Somos cinco en mi familia, mis padres, mis dos hermanas mayores y yo. Mis padres son bastante serios—mi padre es jugador profesional de ajedrez y mi madre escribe libros en español para niños. Mis hermanas tienen diecisiete años. Ana es mejor estudiante que Alicia, pero Alicia es tan inteligente como Ana. Las dos son muy simpáticas y les gusta mucho leer.
Yo tengo quince años. Soy bastante alto y rubio y tengo los ojos azules. Me gusta estudiar biología y física, montar en bicicleta, jugar al béisbol y leer. Leo casi tantos libros como mis hermanas. Me levanto a las siete todas las mañanas y me acuesto a las diez todas las noches, excepto el sábado, cuando prefiero levantarme tarde y acostarme tarde. Quiero estudiar medicina en el futuro y pienso trabajar en un país hispanohablante.
Escríbeme pronto, si puedes. Quiero saber cómo es tu vida en Perú.

Saludos,
Lorenzo

---

1 Where is Lorenzo writing this letter?
A Spain
B Peru
C the United States
D Mexico

2 What does Lorenzo's father do for a living?
F He's a chess teacher.
G He's a chess player.
H He's a chess coach.
J He's a chess judge.

3 How does Lorenzo rank in the family?
A He is the most intelligent.
B He is the oldest.
C He is the youngest.
D He is the most serious.

4 When does Lorenzo's routine change?
F Saturday only
G both Saturday and Sunday
H neither Saturday or Sunday
J Sunday only

5 Which class does Lorenzo probably enjoy most?
A Spanish
B creative writing
C psychology
D science

B Read the following postcard from Catalina to her friend Teodoro. Then choose the best ending for each statement that follows.

México, D.F., jueves, 28 de diciembre
¡Hola, Teodoro!

Estoy en el Paseo de la Reforma, una calle importante y bonita en una de la ciudades más grandes del mundo. Esta mañana voy a la Catedral Metropolitana en la plaza grande, el Zócalo, y luego pienso ir al Museo Nacional de Antropología, donde quiero ver artefactos *(artifacts)* de Tenochtitlán, la antigua capital de los aztecas que es ahora la capital de los mexicanos. Esta tarde voy a los jardines flotantes *(floating)* de Xochimilco a celebrar la quinceañera de mi prima. ¡Tengo muchas ganas de verla!

¡Sé bueno!
Catalina

6 According to the postcard, the Paseo de la Reforma is a street that is
F busy.
G dangerous.
H long.
J beautiful.

7 Catalina says that Tenochtitlán is a
A city.
B lake.
C museum.
D den.

8 According to the postcard, Catalina is going to celebrate
F outside.
G in a restaurant.
H at her cousin's house.
J at home.

9 The term **quinceañera** refers to a
A fruit tree.
B New Year's resolution.
C grade in school.
D birthday party.

10 When it comes to seeing her cousin, Catalina is
F in a hurry.
G afraid.
H eager.
J nervous.

READING   **CAPÍTULO 1**

C Read the following ad from a local newspaper. Then choose the best ending for each statement that follows.

> **¡Vamos a México!**
> **Viajes Covarrubias**
> Goya 45, Madrid
>
> **¿Qué quieres hacer en tus próximas vacaciones?**
> **¡México, D.F., tiene de todo!**
>
> **¿Te gusta conocer el centro de una ciudad o ir de compras?**
> El Paseo de la Reforma es tan interesante como los bulevares de París.
> **¿Te encanta la historia?**
> Visita el Zócalo, una plaza que fue construida sobre las pirámides y los
> palacios de Moctezuma, el emperador azteca que fue conquistado por Cortés.
> **¿Prefieres el arte contemporáneo?**
> Puedes ver los murales de Diego Rivera y las pinturas de Frida Kahlo aquí.
> **Al final de un día de turismo, ¿tienes ganas de relajarte un poco?**
> Prueba un helado o un pastel. *¡Chocolate* viene de una palabra azteca!
>
> Llámanos al 812 65 88 para saber cómo, cuándo y cuánto cuesta ir a
> **¡México!**

11 According to the ad, the Paseo de la Reforma is a good place for
A shopping.
B movies.
C bowling.
D dinner.

12 According to the ad, **Moctezuma** refers to a(n)
F palace.
G conqueror.
H pyramid.
J emperor.

13 Diego Rivera and Frida Kahlo probably created art that is
A from the Renaissance.
B classical.
C modern.
D abstract.

14 According to the ad, a dessert at the end of the day helps the tourist
F gain weight.
G relax.
H cool off.
J improve his or her energy.

15 **Viajes Covarrubias** tells the reader to
A get information on their Web site.
B call for information.
C write for information.
D find information in the library.

Complete the following tasks in writing.

16 Imagine that you are spending the summer in Mexico City and that you want to tell a friend about the people you are meeting. Write an e-mail in Spanish describing the family with whom you are living. List some of their routines and likes and dislikes, and then compare your habits and preferences with theirs.

17 Imagine that you have been to Mexico City and that you are helping your Spanish teacher organize a class trip there. Write a letter in English to the parents of your classmates describing what the class will see and do there and how the trip will help all of you with your classwork. Be sure to use some of the information about Mexico City you learned in this chapter.

18 Imagine that you are a writer for the school newspaper. Write an interview in Spanish in which you ask an exchange student from Mexico City to compare his or her life here with life in Mexico City.

En el vecindario

A Read the following e-mail from Maura to her friend Julia. Then, choose the best ending for each statement that follows.

¡Hola, Julia!

¿Qué tal? ¿Tienes que estudiar mucho en la universidad? ¿Te gusta tu compañera de cuarto (*roommate*)? ¿Cómo son tus profesores? ¿Te ayudan mucho?

Mis padres me dicen que debo pensar en mi futura profesión. Yo les digo que tengo sólo dieciocho años, que ahora quiero estudiar y salir con mis amigos. ¿Qué piensas tú? ¿Tengo que ser tan seria?

Tienen razón mis padres. Pero ¿a qué trabajo me dedico? ¿Quiero ser médica como mi madre? ¿Me gustaría ser carpintera como mi padre? ¿Puedo diseñar lámparas y muebles como mi hermana o páginas Web como mi hermano? Mi prima enseña a niños bilingües. Me encantaría ayudar a la gente usando mis dos idiomas. Quiero hacer algo por mi barrio y mi país.

Cuídate, Julia, ¡y hazme el favor de escribirme muy pronto!

Maura

---

1 According to this e-mail, Julia is
  A just beginning high school.
  B about to graduate from high school.
  C in college.
  D a recent college graduate.

2 Maura reacts to her parents' advice by indicating that she wants to
  F have fun.
  G leave home.
  H get a weekend job.
  J move in with friends.

3 According to the e-mail, Maura's brother is probably a(n)
  A doctor.
  B carpenter.
  C artist.
  D programmer.

4 Maura says that she wants to make use of her
  F social skills.
  G vocational classes.
  H computer knowledge.
  J language abilities.

5 Maura asks for Julia's
  A concern.
  B advice.
  C address.
  D agreement.

B Read the following postcard from Jaime and Rosa to their grandfather. Then, choose the best answer for each question that follows.

Querido Abuelito,

Es el quince de diciembre. Llegamos a Cuzco, la antigua capital del Imperio Inca, anoche muy tarde. ¡Dormimos bien! Hoy fuimos a la iglesia de Santo Domingo, que antes fue el Templo del Sol, un lugar sagrado de los incas. Después, fuimos a la Plaza de Armas, que antes fue el *huacapata* o la plaza central de los incas. En un mercado enfrente de la plaza, te compramos una cerámica cuzqueña que combina los diseños incaicos y españoles, y una vela. Cenamos papas y maíz típicos de este país. Nos gustó todo. ¡Hasta pronto! ¡Te queremos mucho!

Jaime y Rosa

---

6 According to the postcard, why did Jaime and Rosa go to bed late on Saturday?
   F They went to the movies.
   G They shopped all day.
   H They had just arrived in the city.
   J They went sightseeing.

7 What did Jaime and Rosa say that the **huacapata** was?
   A a Spanish fort
   B an Incan temple
   C a Spanish market
   D an Incan town square

8 Where is the market that Jaime and Rosa visited in relation to the **Plaza de Armas?**
   F near the plaza
   G in front of the plaza
   H far away from the plaza
   J inside the plaza

9 Whose influence is shown in Cuzco ceramics?
   A the Incas' only
   B the Incas' and the Spaniards'
   C the Spaniards' only
   D neither the Incas' nor the Spaniards'

10 What typical Peruvian food did Jaime and Rosa have for dinner?
   F vegetables
   G desserts
   H soft drinks
   J seafood

C Read the following ad from a local newspaper. Then, choose the best ending for each statement that follows.

Centro comercial «Los cuzqueños»

Eléctricodomésticos León tiene los últimos modelos de refrigeradores, estufas, lavaplatos, lavadoras y secadoras para los quehaceres de cada día.

Casa Buena ofrece una gran selección de sofás, sillones, mesas, sillas, mesitas, cómodas, estantes y televisores para cada habitación.

Uniformes Nicolás vende ropa para policías, bomberos, carteros, mecánicos, médicos y mucho más.

Salón de Belleza Alto Estilo quiere servirte con los mejores peluqueros de la ciudad. Les dan la bienvenida a hombres y mujeres, niños y niñas.

Escuela Buen Viaje te prepara para el examen de conducir. Si quieres conducir tu coche privado o ser conductor profesional de camiones, te ayudamos a conseguir el permiso oficial.

---

11 According to the ad, the **León** store sells
   A furniture.
   B plumbing supplies.
   C home repair kits.
   D appliances.

12 According to the ad, **Casa Buena** probably has very few items for the
   F kitchen.
   G dining room.
   H living room.
   J bedroom.

13 The **Nicolás** store probably sells
   A boots.
   B wigs.
   C brooms.
   D tools.

14 According to the ad, **Alto Estilo** serves
   F only men and boys.
   G only adults.
   H adults and children.
   J only women and girls.

15 **Buen Viaje** offers help in obtaining
   A parking permits.
   B driver's licenses.
   C trucks or cars.
   D tour-guide positions.

Complete the following task in writing.

16 Imagine that you write a career column for a local newspaper and that a student has asked you for advice about choosing a trade or profession. Write an article in Spanish recommending possible job opportunities, based on the student's background and interests.

17 Imagine that you have an opportunity to travel with a student group to Cuzco and that you need to convince your parents to let you go. Write a note in English to them telling three or four things you will do there and explain two or three ways your experiences will benefit you. Use some of the information you learned about Cuzco in this chapter.

18 Imagine that you have just spent the summer with a family in Cuzco and that your Spanish teacher has asked you to tell the class about your experiences. Write an interview in Spanish including what your teacher might ask you and how you might answer. Mention three or four things you did while you were there, including leisure activities, shopping trips, and special occasions.

Pueblos y ciudades

A Read the following speech that Felipe has given for a contest. Then choose the best ending for each statement that follows.

Mi Pueblo

¿Quieres pasearte conmigo por mi pueblo? No es grande pero es bonito y tiene todo lo que se necesita. Bajamos a la plaza por estas calles calladas. ¿Tienes hambre? Hay una pastelería y una heladería muy buenas y se puede comer en una banca en la acera y mirar la fuente. ¿O prefieres ese café que está en la esquina, donde se ve bien el monumento a Pedro Mir, el poeta nacional dominicano? Después te llevo al centro recreativo y al mercado, donde se puede encontrar quioscos que venden arte, flores, periódicos, libros y muebles.

Tengo que hacer unas diligencias aquí. Vamos a la pescadería y a la frutería. Te preparo una sopa de mariscos y luego tenemos naranjas y algo de postre y charlamos. Mañana pienso llevarte al acuario que está cerca del puerto. Luego damos una vuelta por el cementerio, que tiene una vista (view) fantástica del pueblo.

Así vamos a pasarlo bien en mi pueblo.

---

1 In the description, Felipe asks the reader to go with him on a
 A boat ride.
 B bicycle trip.
 C bus ride.
 D walk.

2 Felipe says his town offers
 F everything.
 G many things.
 H nothing.
 J some things.

3 According to Felipe, a good place to see the fountain is from a
 A bank.
 B café.
 C bench.
 D market.

4 Felipe says that the market sells
 F cheese.
 G newspapers.
 H magazines.
 J pastries.

5 The **sopa** that Felipe prepares is probably very fresh because he
 A bought it yesterday.
 B lives near the sea.
 C found it at an aquarium.
 D asked a neighbor for it.

B Read the following postcard from Paloma to her grandparents. Then choose the best answer for each question that follows.

viernes, 4 de enero

Queridos abuelos,
Llegué a Santo Domingo ayer para pasar cuatro meses
en un colegio aquí. Fui primero a la residencia de
estudiantes y luego una amiga me recogió y nos
subimos al autobús para ir a la clínica y al ayuntamiento.
Pasamos por la Avenida George Washington, o el
Malecón, y vimos el mar Caribe por un lado. Hicimos
las diligencias y luego visitamos el impresionante
Alcázar de Colón, que fue construido por Diego Colón,
el hijo de Cristóbal. Fuimos también a la Plaza de la
Cultura a ver museos y cenamos habichuelas con dulce.
Vengan pronto a conocer esta ciudad.

Su nieta que los adora,
Paloma

6 Why does Paloma say that she is in Santo Domingo?
   F to go to school
   G to volunteer at a clinic
   H to swim in the Caribbean
   J to work at city hall

7 How did Paloma get to City Hall?
   F She rode a bicycle.
   G She walked.
   H She took a taxi.
   J She took a bus.

8 What is the Malecón in Santo Domingo?
   A a supermarket
   B a name for the cathedral
   C a name for an avenue
   D a museum

9 What did Paloma see at the Plaza de la Cultura?
   A the sea
   B a museum
   C a theater
   D a restaurant

10 What does Paloma ask her grandparents to do?
   F write to her
   G never forget her
   H send her a swimsuit
   J visit Santo Domingo

READING

C Read the flyer. Then choose the best ending for each statement that follows.

¡Fiesta de fin del año para el vecindario del centro!
Celebren Uds. el Año Nuevo
en el Centro Recreativo «Boca Chica» de Santo Domingo,
sábado, 31 de diciembre.

¡Organicen un grupo de amigos, salgan de la casa, vengan a la playa!
¡Bailen, canten, coman!
Vamos a estar aquí con el grupo musical «República»
desde las 9 de la noche hasta las 3 de la mañana.
El costo, que incluye música, comida y bebidas, es sólo $20 por persona.

El Centro «Boca Chica» es nuevo.
¿Saben Uds. cómo pueden llegar? Es muy fácil.

Desde el norte en la carretera 4-SD, vayan a la salida *(exit)* 12.
Doblen a la derecha en la Avenida Duarte y sigan derecho tres cuadras.
En el cruce entre Duarte y la Calle de Colón, doblen a la izquierda.
Pasen por dos semáforos y busquen el Centro en Palmira, 22.
Hay estacionamiento entre el Centro y la Comisaría Central.
Si se pierden, nuestro teléfono es el 543 5432.

¡Nos vemos pronto!

---

11 According to the flyer, the New Year's party in Santo Domingo is for people who live in the
  A country.
  B downtown area.
  C new area.
  D outskirts of the city.

12 República probably refers to a
  F welcoming committee.
  G kiosk for party hats.
  H pastry vendor.
  J band.

13 According to the directions, the Center is
  A easy to find.
  B hard to find.
  C very old.
  D far from the parking lot.

14 According to the directions, after the reader is on Duarte Avenue, he or she
  F continues several blocks.
  G turns to the right.
  H goes to the end of the street.
  J goes through some traffic lights.

15 The flyer includes the telephone number of the Center in case the reader
  A wants to reserve a table.
  B gets lost on the way.
  C needs a parking permit.
  D has any meal requests.

WRITING   CAPÍTULO 3

Complete the following tasks in writing.

16 Imagine that you have just arrived in Santo Domingo for the school year and that you have to run some errands. Write four complete sentences in Spanish describing in order four things you need to buy and do, and where you need to go.

17 Imagine that you live in Santo Domingo and that you want to show the city to a friend who has never visited it before. Write an e-mail in English describing to your friend three or four places you will take him or her. Use some of the information you learned about Santo Domingo in this chapter.

18 Imagine that you need to get a haircut and that you don't know how to get to the salon. Write a conversation in Spanish in which you explain your situation to someone on the street and he or she gives you directions.

¡Mantente en forma!

A Read the following entry from Carmen's diary. Then choose the best ending for each statement that follows.

Querido diario,

Estoy muy contenta esta noche. Como sabes, mi equipo y yo fuimos a la competencia nacional de natación en Miami la semana pasada. Todo nos fue muy bien. Nuestra entrenadora nos dijo hoy que ganamos un trofeo como mejor equipo y que Sara, Juana, Laura y yo ganamos trofeos en los eventos individuales. Nos dio tanta alegría que todas nos pusimos a gritar y a reírnos. Luego nos dieron ganas de divertirnos y decidimos ir a la heladería «Polo Norte». La entrenadora no fue con nosotras. Cuando llegó a casa después del viaje desde Miami, se cayó en la acera, se torció el tobillo y se rompió la muñeca. En este momento no puede andar sin ayuda y está muy cansada. ¡Pobrecita! El verano pasado yo tuve una muñeca rota y me sentí horrible. Yo sé muy bien lo que le pasa a la señora ahora.
Bueno, tengo que acostarme. No me dormí hasta las dos esta mañana porque estuve en una fiesta con la familia.

---

1 According to the entry, Carmen went to Miami for a
   A flower show.
   B spelling bee.
   C band contest.
   D swim meet.

2 Carmen went to Miami with her
   F team.
   G list.
   H family.
   J homework.

3 The number of trophies won was
   A five.
   B four.
   C three.
   D two.

4 After hearing the news, Carmen and her friends
   F smiled politely.
   G began to shout.
   H felt like crying.
   J finished their homework.

5 On her return from Miami, the coach
   A broke her wrist.
   B went for ice cream.
   C had her tonsils out.
   D went to a family gathering.

READING

B Read the following postcard from Leandro to his mother. Then choose the best answer for each question that follows.

> martes, 11 de marzo
>
> Querida Mamá,
>
> Aquí estoy en Miami, en la costa atlántica. ¿Sabes que esta ciudad fue fundada en 1896 por una mujer, Julia Tuttle? Ayer fui a Freedom Tower, por donde entraron en este país muchos emigrantes cubanos. Esta tarde voy al Festival de la Calle Ocho para divertirme y aprender más de la cultura cubana. Luego me gustaría hacer windsurf, pero no puedo porque me quemé con el sol ayer y estoy bastante mal. ¡Hasta pronto!
>
> Tu hijo,
> Leandro

6 Where is Miami located?
 F on the coast of the Gulf of Mexico
 G on the Pacific coast
 H on the Atlantic coast
 J on the Mediterranean coast

7 What role did Julia Tuttle play in Miami's history?
 A She was its mayor.
 B She was its historian.
 C She was its founder.
 D She was its architect.

8 Why does Leandro want to go to the Festival de Calle Ocho?
 F to have fun
 G to shop
 H to see a movie
 J to windsurf

9 How was the Freedom Tower used by the Cuban emigrants?
 A as an entrance to the U.S.
 B as a temporary shelter
 C as an exit from the U.S.
 D as a Little Havana

10 Why can't Leandro go wind surfing?
 F He's not good at it.
 G He's too sick to do it.
 H He can't afford it.
 J He can't swim.

C Read the following ad from a local newspaper. Then choose the best ending for each statement that follows.

Consultorio del Arturo Robles

Señor o Señora:
¿Qué tal está su salud *(health)*?

¿Puede decir que «no» a todas las preguntas que siguen?
¿Se enferma regularmente?
¿Se resfría con frecuencia?
¿Tiene dolores de cabeza que no se le quitan?
Cuando se lastima,
¿sigue teniendo dolores por mucho tiempo?

Si dijo que «no» a todas las preguntas, ¡muy bien!
Si dijo que «sí» a una pregunta o más,
¡necesita atención médica!

Llámeme al 555 3456, Calle Ocho 2437, Miami.

---

11 In the context of the ad, **consultorio** probably refers to a
  A doctor's office.
  B sports arena.
  C medical laboratory.
  D fitness center.

12 The ad has mostly to do with how the reader feels
  F mentally.
  G emotionally.
  H spiritually.
  J physically.

13 The ad asks the reader if he or she has headaches that
  A last only a short time.
  B won't go away.
  C happen every week.
  D happen only occasionally.

14 The ad asks the reader if he or she heals quickly from
  F colds.
  G cuts.
  H allergies.
  J headaches.

15 Judging by the ad, the **consultorio** is probably staffed by
  A three doctors.
  B a doctor and a lab technician.
  C a doctor.
  D a visiting consultant.

Complete the following tasks in writing.

16 Imagine that you are on a speech, debate, or sports team and that your group has just lost an important competition. Write an e-mail in Spanish to a friend describing how you and your teammates reacted to the loss.

17 Imagine that you are in Miami and that you are interested in festivals and sports. Write a postcard in English to a friend describing what you did yesterday and what you are planning to do later. Use some of the information you learned about Miami in this chapter.

18 Imagine that you have just fallen and that you are in an emergency room in Miami. Write a dialogue in Spanish describing to the doctor where you were when the accident happened, how it happened, and how you feel now. Also include the advice the doctor gives you.

Día a día

A Read the following e-mail from Susana to her friend Raquel. Then choose the best ending for each statement that follows.

> ¡Hola, Raquel!
>
> Es sábado y quiero divertirme. El fin de semana pasado no hice nada más que trabajar. El sábado mi madre se fue temprano a enseñar una clase de guitarra y yo me levanté a las ocho. Le di de comer al perro, limpié mi cuarto y desperté a Delia, mi hermana menor. Desayunamos, me duché y me arreglé. Luego bañé a Delia, la vestí y la peiné. Conversamos un poco sobre cómo cuidar a una mascota. Después yo hice ejercicios aeróbicos y ella leyó mis revistas cómicas. Por fin llegó mi madre y trajo el almuerzo. Luego estudié por la noche y todo el domingo para los exámenes finales y no vi a nadie. Perdóname, no quiero aburrirte con mi cuento, pero es que me cansé de estar en casa y ahora pienso disfrutar del rato libre que tengo.
> ¿Qué te interesa hacer hoy? ¿Te llama la atención la exhibición de vestidos de gala en el museo? ¿Quieres ver la nueva película de Johnny Depp? Hace mucho tiempo que no vamos al cine.
> Bueno, date prisa y llámame. ¡Se nos hace tarde y quiero divertirme un poco!
>
> Susana

1 Susana tells Raquel that she worked all
   A day yesterday.
   B last week.
   C last weekend.
   D last year.

2 According to the e-mail, Susana's mother taught
   F knitting.
   G music.
   H sewing.
   J martial arts.

3 According to the e-mail, Delia
   A bathed on her own.
   B was bathed by Susana.
   C bathed Susana.
   D did not bathe at all.

4 When the girls' mother came home, she
   F brought lunch.
   G walked the dog.
   H prepared lunch.
   J washed the dog.

5 Susana probably thinks that
   A movies are boring.
   B she should take care of her responsibilities first and have fun later.
   C it's unfair that she has to take care of her little sister.
   D she should go out with her friends first and do her homework later.

B Read the following postcard from Cristóbal to his friend Joaquín. Then choose the best answer for each statement that follows.

San José, Costa Rica, 26 de diciembre

¿Qué tal, Joaquín?

Te escribo desde la capital, que está en un valle cerca de cerros y volcanes. ¿Sabes que San José fue una de las primeras ciudades del mundo en tener luces en las calles y teléfonos públicos? Ayer fuimos al hermoso Jardín de Mariposas Spirogyra y vimos en el Museo Nacional unas piedras perfectamente redondas de los tiempos precolombinos. Ahora tengo que darme prisa porque acaba de llamar Jorge, un amigo mío. Vamos al Parque La Sabana a nadar.

¡Nos vemos en enero!
Cristóbal

6 Where is the capital of Costa Rica located?
F in a valley
G on several hills
H far away from any volcanoes
J in a national forest

7 What was San José one of the earliest cities to have?
A public restrooms
B public parks
C street lights
D national museums

8 When are the stones in the National Museum from?
F from the last fifty years
G from the last hundred years
H from colonial times
J from before the explorers arrived

9 Which statement is the (implied) main idea of the postcard?
A There's a lot to do in San José.
B San José is a very modern city.
C San José is near volcanoes.
D San José is boring.

10 What attraction does Parque La Sabana probably have?
F a market
G a parade
H a pool
J a theater

C Read the following ad from a student newspaper. Then choose the best answer for each statement that follows.

Club de pasatiempos
Escuela Juan Santamaría

¿Te cansas de estudiar todo el tiempo?
¿Quieres practicar algo viejo o aprender algo nuevo?
Ven al Club de pasatiempos
los viernes a las cuatro de la tarde.

Si te gusta...
trabajar con las manos: cose o teje o trabaja en mecánica en el club.
coleccionar cosas: investiga nuestros álbumes de estampillas y monedas.
escuchar música: toca la guitarra o el violín o graba CDs en el club.
producir arte: pinta o diseña páginas Web con nosotros.
jugar con las palabras: escribe poemas o haz crucigramas en el club.

Si te gusta divertirte en los ratos libres, con gente interesante,
¡Somos tu club!

Para más información, habla con el señor Benítez en 141.

---

11 **Pasatiempos** probably refers to
  A part-time jobs.
  B earlier times.
  C hobbies.
  D schedules.

12 According to the ad, joining the club will give the reader
  F better grades.
  G enjoyment.
  H new card tricks.
  J headaches.

13 There is an opportunity in the club for the reader to
  A play a musical instrument.
  B work with clay.
  C take photographs.
  D play cards.

14 According to the ad, the club attracts people who are
  F interesting.
  G boring.
  H optimistic.
  J pessimistic.

15 The statement that best summarizes this ad is
  A this is a club for people only interested in sports.
  B this is a club for people only interested in politics.
  C this is a club for people who want to do different hobbies.
  D this is a club for people who need help with homework.

Complete the following tasks in writing.

16 Imagine that you have made a new friend in school who shares two of your outside-of-school interests. Write an e-mail in Spanish to a relative telling what interests you and your new friend have in common and what you two have planned for the next time you get together.

17 Imagine that you are with a friend who lives in San José and that he or she spent all day yesterday taking you to places in the city. Write a letter in English to a friend describing three or four places you went. Use some of the information you learned about San José in this chapter.

18 Imagine that you are having lunch with friends and that one of your parents calls to check on what you did before you left home today. Write a conversation in Spanish that includes what your parent asks and how you answer.

MATH TEST 1

The distances on the chart below are given in either kilometers or miles. Use the formula M = k × .62 to convert kilometers to miles, or K = m ÷ .62 to convert miles to kilometers.
(M = distance in miles; K = distance in kilometers) Round to the nearest kilometer or mile, as the case may be.

Distancias entre ciudades: España

Ciudades	distancia en kilómetros	distancia en millas
Ávila–Burgos	243	
Barcelona–Córdoba		271
Cáceres–Gerona	1018	
Cádiz–Granada	335	
León–Almería	896	
Santander–Oviedo		128
Zaragoza–Lérida		87

1 ¿Cuál es la distancia en millas entre León y Almería?
A 535 m
B 545 m
C 556 m
D 565 m

2 ¿Cuál es la distancia en kilómetros entre Zaragoza y Lérida?
F 125 km
G 140 km
H 155 km
J 170 km

3 ¿Cuál es la distancia en kilómetros entre Barcelona y Córdoba?
A 407 km
B 422 km
C 437 km
D 452 km

4 ¿Cuál es la distancia en millas entre Ávila y Burgos?
F 151 m
G 161 m
H 171 m
J 181 m

5 ¿Cuál es la distancia en millas entre Cádiz y Granada?
A 198 mi
B 208 mi
C 218 mi
D 228 mi

Read each question and choose the best answer. Then mark the letter for the answer you have chosen.

6 Si tienes dos dados *(dice)*, ¿cuál es la probabilidad de tirar *(roll)* un total de 10?
   F 1/12
   G 1/18
   H 1/24
   J 1/36

7 Había 1000 estudiantes en la escuela de Daniel. El 10 por ciento de los estudiantes llegaron hoy en bicicleta y el 25 por ciento llegaron en autobús. ¿Cuántos estudiantes llegaron por otro medio *(means)* de transporte?
   A 350
   B 600
   C 650
   D 750

8 La longitud *(length)* de una mesita es el doble de su ancho *(width)*. El perímetro es 48 cm. ¿Cuál es su longitud?
   F 8 cm
   G 12 cm
   H 16 cm
   J 20 cm

9 Dos números consecutivos tienen una suma *(sum)* de 191. ¿Cuál es el número mayor?
   A 91
   B 93
   C 95
   D 96

10 Juan nació en abril y Elena también nació en abril. ¿Cuál es la probabilidad de ocurrir los dos cumpleaños en la misma fecha?
   F 1/7
   G 1/12
   H 1/30
   J 12/30

Recuerdos

A Read the following letter that Mariana has put on the class bulletin board. Then, choose the best answer for each question that follows.

> Querida Mariana,
>
> Me preguntaste qué hacía de pequeña y qué quería ser. En los años 50, me divertía mucho jugando en el patio o en el jardín. Mi familia tenía televisor, pero sólo había programas en blanco y negro y eso me aburría. Tenía una radio, pero toda la música en aquel entonces era la música de mis padres. Elvis llegó unos años más tarde y nos dio a los jóvenes una música propia. Bueno, había muchos niños en el vecindario y nos veíamos todo el tiempo. Nos peleábamos a veces pero casi siempre nos llevábamos bien. En el verano, trepábamos a los árboles, jugábamos al escondite y de noche nos contábamos cuentos de terror. Siempre me interesaban los cuentos, pero uno me molestó tanto que no pude dormir por dos días y no quise salir de casa. En el invierno, yo pasaba muchas horas solitarias en mi cuarto, donde jugaba con mis bloques y mis muñecas, leía y estudiaba. El programa espacial de Estados Unidos me fascinaba y soñaba con ser astronauta. Más tarde estudié ciencias en la universidad, pero no fui a la Luna. Ahora soy profesora de química y me siento muy contenta.
>
> Con cariño,
> Tía Gracia

1 What did Mariana ask Gracia about?
A high school
B childhood
C church or temple
D vacations

2 Why didn't Gracia like television?
F It had too many Westerns.
G Her mother made her go outside.
H The music was too loud.
J It wasn't in color.

3 What does Gracia says about her relationship with her young neighbors?
A They fought all the time.
B They never fought.
C They hated each other.
D They generally got along well.

4 What did one of the terror stories that Gracia heard cause her to do?
F to write her own
G to cry
H to lose sleep
J to scare the neighbors

5 How does Gracia feel about not being an astronaut?
A She is happy doing something else.
B She is angry that she is not one.
C Fine. She is teaching history instead.
D Awful. She is looking for a job.

B Read the following postcard from Jaime to his friend Ramón. Then, choose the best ending for each statement that follows.

Segovia, sábado, 31 de mayo

¿Qué tal, Ramón?

Llegué hoy en el tren que vino de Madrid. Desayuné cerca del acueducto romano, una construcción de arcos que llevaba agua a Segovia por dos mil años. Después fui al Alcázar, un palacio que está situado sobre unas rocas altas donde se juntan *(join)* los ríos Clamores y Eresma. Las torres hermosas me hicieron pensar en el cuento de la «Bella Durmiente». Supe que Isabel, la reina que le dio dinero a Colón para su famoso viaje, fue coronada en el palacio. Hice mucho hoy y voy a dormir bien esta noche.

Hasta pronto,
Jaime

6 According to the postcard, the train in which Jaime traveled probably arrived in Segovia
F at night.
G in the afternoon.
H in the morning.
J late.

7 The aqueduct in Segovia supplied the city with water for two
A thousand years.
B centuries.
C purposes.
D palaces.

8 The palace Jaime mentions was probably built
F last year.
G 100 years ago.
H 200 years ago.
J more than 500 years ago.

9 According to Jaime, the palace he saw was called the
A Eresma.
B Colón.
C Clamores.
D Alcázar.

10 The statement that best summarizes this text is
F Segovia is a modern industrial city.
G Segovia is a city with several interesting historical attractions.
H Segovia is not worth visiting.
J touring Segovia can make you tired.

C Read the following ad from a local newspaper. Then, choose the best ending for each statement that follows.

¿Te acuerdas de cuando tú...

eras pequeño y casi odiabas a tu hermano mayor?
eras bueno y él siempre hacía travesuras?
coleccionabas láminas y él coleccionaba insectos?
eras callado y él era conversador?
eras paciente y él era impaciente?
jugabas a las damas y él echaba carreras?
eras bondadoso y él era egoísta y le fastidiaba compartir?

Bueno, ¡la vida cambia!
Tu hermano es médico,
colecciona fotos de animales en peligro (*endangered*),
habla con sus pacientes de una manera amable y los escucha,
juega a la casita con sus tres hijas,
y quiere oír de ti.

Tu hermano es buena gente. ¿Por qué no lo llamas esta noche?

Compañía Segovia
Servicio telefónico para ti y tu familia

---

11 The ad first encourages the reader to
   A remember.
   B take notes.
   C forget.
   D read music.

12 The ad implies that the two brothers
   F had similar interests.
   G played with each other's toys.
   H had similar personalities.
   J were quite different.

13 The ad indicates that the older brother
   A found a job in a zoo.
   B changed as an adult.
   C lost his patience.
   D lost his hearing.

14 The main idea of this ad is that
   F brothers never get along well.
   G people never change.
   H you should stay in touch with your family.
   J telephone calls are expensive.

15 The ad is probably meant to stimulate
   A train travel.
   B sales of medical supplies.
   C telephone use.
   D souvenir purchases.

Complete the following tasks in writing.

16 Imagine that you have just heard about an important event in your family, school, or country and that you want to remember it for a long time. Write a diary entry in Spanish telling what happened, where and how you found about about it, and how you felt.

17 Imagine that you are with a school group in Spain and that you really like Segovia. Write an e-mail in English to a friend describing two or three things about the natural setting of the city and one or two things about the way the buildings look. Use some of the information you learned about Segovia in this chapter.

18 Imagine that you have visited several important historical sites in Segovia and that you want to call home to tell your family about what you have seen, but your cell phone isn't working. Write a conversation in Spanish in which you ask someone for directions to the nearest telephone service company. In the conversation, explain why you need to make a phone call.

¡Buen provecho!

A Read the following e-mail from Zoraida to her friend Lucinda. Then choose the best ending for each statement that follows.

¡Hola, Lucinda!

Ayer mis padres y yo cenamos en el restaurante Estrellas. El mesero nos trajo el menú enseguida y nos dijo de las especialidades de la casa. También nos recomendó el té con menta *(mint),* pero sólo queríamos el agua mineral. Luego mi papá pidió el bistec encebollado, mi mamá los mariscos con vegetales y yo el pollo asado con gandules. Yo quería almendras y tomates picados y me los añadió. Mientras se preparaban los platos principales, probamos un gazpacho con trozos de cebollas y ajíes crudos. Estaba fresco y sabroso. Un violinista tocaba y conversábamos tranquilamente hasta que nos sirvieron los platos, que estaban perfectamente cocidos. De postre comimos un flan de vainilla que estaba un poco aguado y sabía a flan congelado. Mi papá pagó la cuenta, dejó la propina y nos dijo que la próxima vez no iba a pedir postre. Me gustó Estrellas y te lo recomiendo, pero ahora quiero comida rápida. ¿Quieres ir al café Hamburguesa Celestial? A veces necesito algo frito y salado. ¡Qué rico va a estar!

Hasta pronto,
Zoraida

1 The family received menus
  A after a long wait.
  B at the door.
  C right away.
  D after a short wait.

2 Zoraida says that she ordered
  F iced tea.
  G mineral water.
  H cold milk.
  J hot tea.

3 The (implied) main idea of the text is that
  A Zoraida's favorite kind of food is fast food.
  B Estrellas is a good restaurant.
  C Estrellas is not a good restaurant.
  D the desserts at Estrellas are not good.

4 The following detail that supports the main idea is that
  F the dessert at Estrellas was not very good.
  G the **gazpacho** was fresh and delicious.
  H Zoraida ordered mineral water.
  J Zoraida sometimes likes to eat fast food.

5 The statement that does not support the main idea is that
  A the flan at Estrellas was a little watery and tasted like it had been frozen.
  B the main courses at Estrellas were cooked perfectly.
  C the waiter at Estrellas brought the menus right away.
  D Zoraida recommends Estrellas to Lucinda.

B Read the following postcard from Patricio to his friend Roberto. Then choose the best answer for each question that follows.

San Juan, 17 de febrero

¡Hola, Roberto!

Estoy en la capital de Puerto Rico, que fue fundada en 1521 por los españoles. La llamaron la «Ciudad Amurallada» y la usaron como bastión militar. Ayer fui a ver El Morro, una fortaleza construida por los españoles para proteger el puerto de San Juan contra los ataques de otros europeos. Me encantó su laberinto de túneles y puestos de guardia. ¿Te acuerdas de la historia de Ponce de León, el que buscaba la fuente de juventud y descubrió Florida? Fue el primer gobernador de esta isla.

Hasta la próxima semana,
Patricio

6 Why did the Spanish probably build walls around San Juan?
 F for tranquility
 G for solitude
 H for physical protection
 J to create a space for gardens

7 Why was El Morro primarily built?
 A to be used as a fortress
 B to be used as barracks
 C to be used as a hiding place
 D to be used as a landing dock

8 According to the postcard, what did Ponce de León discover?
 F El Morro
 G Florida
 H Puerto Rico
 J the Fountain of Youth

9 What else is Ponce de León known for?
 A being a physicist
 B being a historian
 C being a professor
 D being a governor

10 When Patricio mentions **esta isla,** what is he probably referring to?
 F Cuba
 G Jamaica
 H the Dominican Republic
 J Puerto Rico

C Read the flyer. Then choose the best ending for each statement that follows.

Tienda « ¡Es bueno para usted!»
Calle San Sebastián 19, Teléfono 765 0343

Responda usted brevemente a la siguiente encuesta. Tráiganosla directamente y le ofrecemos un cupón de $15 para usar en la tienda.
1) ¿Cree que lleva una dieta balanceada?

_____

2) ¿Cuántos gramos de carbohidratos consume al día?

_____

3) ¿Cuántos gramos de proteínas consume al día?

_____

4) ¿Cuántos gramos de grasas consume al día?

_____

5) ¿Es su dieta carnívora, vegetariana o vegetariana estricta?

_____

6) ¿Qué usa para añadir sabor a su comida: especias, aceites o salsas?

_____

7) ¿Le recomienda su médico o médica suplementos para su dieta?

_____

¡Le damos las gracias por su ayuda!

---

11 This store probably specializes in
 A healthful food.
 B exercise gear.
 C medical equipment.
 D telephone accessories.

12 The respondent will receive a coupon by
 F mailing in the form.
 G phoning in the answers.
 H taking the form to the store.
 J faxing the replies.

13 The word **carnívora** probably refers to
 A eating corn.
 B racing horses.
 C eating meat.
 D growing crops.

14 The ad suggests that spices give food
 F color.
 G flavor.
 H texture.
 J moisture.

15 In the context of the ad, the word **suplementos** probably refers to
 A oil and vinegar.
 B sugar-free candy.
 C salt and pepper.
 D vitamin tablets.

Complete the following tasks in writing.

16 Imagine that you have invited a friend to lunch at your house and that you want the meal to be simple and nutritious. Write a note to your friend in Spanish describing the ingredients you will use for the drinks, the sandwiches, the soup or salad, and the dessert. Use some cooking terms and comment on how it will all turn out.

17 Imagine that you are in San Juan and that you want to tell someone about your visit. Write an e-mail in English to a friend describing three or four places you have seen and one or two things you have observed in general. Use some of the information about San Juan you learned in this chapter.

18 Imagine that a friend has asked you for advice about nutrition and that you have recently learned a lot about managing a healthful, balanced diet. Write a conversation in Spanish describing your friend's eating habits and your responses to his or her food choices.

Tiendas y puestos

A Read the following e-mail from Marcela to her friend Laura. Then choose the best ending for each statement that follows.

> ¿Qué tal, Laura?
>
> Todavía estoy en Santiago. Me gusta visitar todos los lugares históricos de aquí pero también me gusta ir de compras. Ayer mi madre y yo tomamos el metro para ir al Mercado Central. Buscábamos regalos allí para mi abuela y mis dos hermanos mayores que no pudieron viajar con nosotros. En el primer puesto vimos una preciosa bufanda de seda para la abuela. Era carísimo y el vendedor no quiso regatear. En el segundo miramos un bonito plato hondo de cerámica. Era muy grande y no sabíamos cómo lo íbamos a llevar a casa. Por fin encontramos un pequeño mantel de encaje. Era bastante caro, unos noventa dólares. Regateamos con el dueño y nos lo rebajó a sesenta. Luego encontramos unos guantes de cuero para Martín que hacen juego con su chaqueta. Para Marta compramos un suéter de lana que está bordado con pequeñas figuras de animales andinos. Te compramos algo también pero sólo te digo ahora que es de plata. Bueno, ¡escríbeme pronto!
>
> Tu amiga,
> Marcela

1 Marcela says that she likes
   A sightseeing more.
   B shopping more.
   C neither sightseeing nor shopping.
   D both sightseeing and shopping.

2 As for making the trip to Santiago, the rest of Marcela's family
   F could not.
   G dared not.
   H refused to.
   J wanted to.

3 Marcela and her mother bought the grandmother a
   A lace tablecloth.
   B a silk scarf.
   C a lace scarf.
   D a ceramic bowl.

4 The gift for Marcela's brother is made of
   F clay.
   G ceramic.
   H leather.
   J gold.

5 The statement that best summarizes the text is
   A everything in the Mercado Central is too expensive.
   B Marcela bought four gifts.
   C Marcela had a successful shopping trip at the Mercado Central.
   D bargaining is always the best way to get good prices.

READING   **CAPÍTULO 8**

B Read the following postcard from Esteban to his friend Rafaela. Then, choose the best answer for each question that follows.

Santiago, viernes, 12 de enero

¡Hola, Rafaela!

Me encuentro hoy en la capital de Chile en el centro del país, al pie de los Andes. Esta mañana anduvimos por el barrio París-Londres, que es una joya de la arquitectura y un monumento histórico. Luego visitamos la Plaza de Armas, el centro histórico de Santiago y el lugar de donde se miden todas las distancias al resto de Chile. De allí fuimos al Parque Metropolitano y subimos al Cerro San Cristóbal a ver una vista panorámica de la ciudad. ¡Esta noche vamos a cenar el rico pescado fresco del Mercado Central!

¡Hasta pronto!
Esteban

---

6 According to the postcard, where is Santiago located?
F high in the Andes
G on top of ancient ruins
H between Paris and London
J in the center of Chile

7 What was Esteban's reaction to the **barrio** he visited?
A He was disappointed.
B He was impressed.
C He was sympathetic.
D He was bored.

8 What is located in the Plaza de Armas?
F the university planetarium
G the public library
H the national military cemetery
J the geographical center of Chile

9 According to the postcard, what does the Cerro San Cristóbal offer?
A a movie theatre
B a carousel ride
C a scenic view
D a hiking trail

10 How does Esteban probably feel about tonight's meal?
F eager
G patient
H indifferent
J sympathetic

Holt Spanish 2   34   **Standardized Assessment Tutor**

C Read the following ad from a local newspaper. Then choose the best ending for each statement that follows.

Tienda «Cielos de Santiago»

¿Conoces este tipo de conversación del probador de ropa?

—¿Cómo me veo con este traje?
—Te ves elegantísimo(a) con el saco pero los pantalones te quedan flojos.
—No quiero probarme otro traje. Sólo me gusta éste, y en este color.
—Bueno, vamos a otra tienda. ¡Va a ser la quinta de esta tarde!

Esa conversación es parte de tu pasado. ¡Encuentra tu futuro en «Cielos»!

Te ofrecemos:
Ropa en tu número y tu color.
Adornos de oro y plata y también de cerámica.
Consejo profesional de los que conocen bien la moda.

Después de una visita a «Cielos»
te miras en el espejo y te dices: ¡Me veo super bien!

Estamos en el barrio Brasil, Avenida Mistral 34, Tel: 342 9063.

---

11 In the dialogue, one person asks how he or she
A stands.
B sits.
C looks.
D walks.

12 The other person says that the
F suit is too small.
G suit is just right.
H pants are baggy.
J jacket is baggy.

13 Besides clothes, «Cielos» sells
A silver accessories.
B woven articles.
C leather goods.
D glass jewelry.

14 The statement that best summarizes the ad is
F «Cielos» offers the lowest prices.
G «Cielos» offers the widest selection.
H «Cielos» sells only brand name clothing.
J «Cielos» offers both formal and casual clothing.

15 According to the ad, shopping at «Cielos» will probably help a person to
A feel healthy.
B look good.
C save money.
D lose weight.

Complete the following tasks in writing.

16 Imagine that you are in Santiago and that you have just bought some decorative items for your room. Write an e-mail in Spanish to a friend describing two or three things you purchased. Also tell where you got them, whether you bargained for the items, or if you paid another price.

17 Imagine that you are in Santiago and that you have just learned about some of its famous landmarks. Write a letter in English to a teacher describing two important places in the city. Use some of the information about Santiago you learned in this chapter.

18 Imagine that you work in a clothing store and that you have just waited on your first customer ever. Write a conversation in Spanish describing how you approached the customer, what he or she asked for, what you answered, and how you ended the transaction.

A nuestro alrededor

A Read the following e-mail from Elisa to her new friend Victoria. Then choose the best answer for each question that follows.

---

martes, 12 de agosto

¡Hola, Victoria!

Recibí tu carta hoy y me dio tanta alegría que quería escribirte enseguida. Me encantó leer las descripciones de tu vida en Segovia. Ahora quiero decirte un poco sobre la mía aquí en Texas. Vivo en un rancho en las afueras de El Paso. Está casi siempre soleado, así que puedo dar caminatas a pie o a caballo regularmente. Es un clima árido pero a veces llueve a cántaros. Hace un mes hubo una tormenta de verano increíble. Estaba montada a caballo y no había ni una nube, ni una brisa. De repente empezaron los truenos y los relámpagos y se cayó un árbol muy cerca de mí. Pero como te dije, generalmente hace sol y puedo gozar de la naturaleza.
Espero que vengas de vacaciones aquí. Montaremos a caballo y podremos ir a pescar en el río. Miraremos las águilas y los buitres. Iremos también a El Paso, que es una ciudad muy interesante del suroeste de Estados Unidos.

Un abrazo,
Elisa

---

1 What does Victoria's letter make Elisa want to do?
 A visit Spain right away
 B send her friend a gift
 C call her friend
 D reply immediately

2 Which statement is the (implied) main idea of the text?
 F It's too hot to go out much.
 G The rainy, cold climate makes outdoor activities difficult.
 H The sunny, dry climate is good for outdoor activities.
 J Elisa enjoys nature, but doesn't like to go outside.

3 What does Elisa say about when it rains on the ranch?
 A It pours down.
 B It scares the animals.
 C It only sprinkles.
 D It goes on for days.

4 How does Elisa enjoy nature?
 F on television
 G from her room
 H on horseback
 J in books

5 What does Elisa plan to do when Victoria comes to visit?
 A go hunting
 B go sailing
 C go canoeing
 D go horseback riding

B Read the following postcard from Gonzalo to his friend Leticia. Then choose the best ending for each statement that follows.

El Paso, 16 de mayo

¡Hola, Leticia!

Estoy en el desierto en el extremo oeste de Texas. Ayer fui a Hueco Tanks a ver unas formaciones de rocas donde vivía la cultura prehistórica Jornada Mogollón. Hoy espero visitar la Capilla de San Elizario, que está hecha de adobe, un tipo de ladrillo muy usado en el suroeste de Estados Unidos. Mañana voy a Fort Bliss, un fuerte militar que es la mayor empresa de aquí. Contribuye más de un millón de dólares cada año a El Paso. Luego iré al Parque Estatal Montañas Franklin. ¡Espero que no haya serpientes allá!

Hasta pronto,
Gonzalo

---

6 According to the postcard, the climate of El Paso is probably
F very dry.
G very moist.
H very windy.
J extremely cold.

7 Jornada Mogollón refers to a
A tank formation.
B human group.
C religious site.
D rock formation.

8 According to the postcard, **adobe** is a kind of
F wood.
G brick.
H plastic.
J metal.

9 The Fort Bliss contribution that Gonzalo mentions probably refers to
A education.
B construction.
C agriculture.
D salaries.

10 On his trip to the state park, Gonzalo would probably not like to run across
F reptiles.
G amphibians.
H birds.
J mammals.

C Read the ad from a local newspaper. Then choose the best ending for each statement that follows.

¿Será ésta tu historia?

Había una vez un chico o una chica que se aburría de la rutina de siempre.
Le parecía que pasaba toda su vida en el colegio y en la casa.
Quería hacer algo más activo, saludable y divertido, pero no sabía qué.

Un día mientras leía el periódico, vio un anuncio *(ad)*. Los Jóvenes
Aventureros buscaban nuevos miembros. El chico o la chica los llamó,
habló unos minutos, apagó el televisor, se puso los zapatos y se fue a una
reunión del grupo. Allá planearon excursiones a los ríos, las montañas y
los bosques. Hablaron de hacer camping, de dar caminatas, de explorar
y de observar. El chico o la chica encontró lo que esperaba, con gente
amable de su edad y cerca de su ciudad.

¿Puede ser ésta tu historia? Llámanos al 688 7623.
¡Te invitamos a formar parte de nuestro grupo!

Jóvenes Aventureros de El Paso

---

11 This ad is probably addressed to the reader who is
   A in a rut.
   B on a budget.
   C in a hurry.
   D on vacation.

12 The person in this ad read an ad, then
   F called a friend.
   G looked at a website.
   H watched television.
   J went to a meeting.

13 Most of the group's activities probably take place in
   A meeting rooms.
   B natural settings.
   C sporting goods stores.
   D gyms or spas.

14 According to this ad, the group offers the reader opportunities for
   F sightseeing only.
   G exercise only.
   H neither sightseeing nor exercise.
   J both sightseeing and exercise.

15 According to this ad, the group probably will not
   A travel across the country.
   B go camping.
   C see mountains.
   D go exploring.

Complete the following tasks in writing.

16 Imagine that you are planning a camping trip with a friend and that the two of you can't agree on where to go. Write an e-mail in Spanish to the friend describing why you prefer one place to the other in terms of weather, setting, and things to do and see.

17 Imagine that you are visiting El Paso and that you want to tell someone about what you've done in the city. Write a postcard in English to a friend describing three or four buildings you've seen. Use some of the information you learned about El Paso in this chapter.

18 Imagine that you are going camping by the ocean with your adventure group and that you need to pack for the trip. Write a conversation in Spanish describing what you are going to do at the shore and asking someone for help in deciding what to take.

De vacaciones

A Read the following e-mail from Julián to his friend David. Then choose the best answer for each question that follows.

¡Hola, David!

Me encantó oír que te han aceptado en el programa de verano en Buenos Aires. ¿Sabías que he participado en él dos veces? Por eso, quiero aconsejarte un poco. Es importante que lleves contigo la dirección y el teléfono de los directores del programa. Tienes que llamarlos para que vayan a recogerte en el aeropuerto. Para llamar, necesitas unas monedas o una tarjeta telefónica. Te sugiero que pidas información sobre esto en un quiosco para turistas. Claro, puedes tomar un taxi si quieres. ¿En dónde vas a hospedarte? Si no has decidido, te recomiendo que te quedes en un dormitorio de la escuela. Te costará menos que un hotel, estarás cerca de tus clases y harás amigos más rápidamente. Irás en excursiones en tus clases, pero en tus ratos libres es buena idea que vayas a la oficina de turismo. Allí puedes conseguir unas guías turísticas y un plano de la ciudad. Espero que me cuentes lo que te pasa allá. Y dales un saludo a los directores de mi parte. ¡Buen viaje!

Un abrazo,
Julián

---

1 What is the main purpose of this letter?
A to ask a favor
B to offer advice
C to send a greeting
D to tell a story

2 What should David do to get a ride from the airport?
F take a taxi
G take a bus
H call one of the directors
J take a taxi or call one of the directors

3 What does Julián suggest that David do if he needs help with a call?
A go to a tourist booth
B talk with the local operator
C use his cell phone
D get advice from a taxi driver

4 Which of the following details supports the main purpose of the letter?
F Julián attended the program twice.
G Julián tells David that he should stay in the school dormitory.
H Julián asks David to greet the teachers for him.
J Julián tells David that he will go on trips with his class.

5 Through David, what does Julián want to send the directors?
A a card
B a hug
C a smile
D a greeting

B Read the following postcard from Damián to his father. Then choose the best ending for each statement that follows.

Buenos Aires, Argentina, 10 de julio

Querido Papá,

Me han puesto en una pensión cerca del Río de la Plata. Ya he hecho unas excursiones buenísimas. Ayer fui a la Casa Rosada, la residencia del presidente del país. También visité el Café Tortoni para ver si había gente famosa. Carlos Gardel, el mejor cantante del tango actual *(of today)* ha estado allí, pero no estuvo anoche. Hoy vi en la Catedral Metropolitana una llama siempre encendida en honor a José de San Martín, el libertador y héroe nacional del país. Mañana espero visitar La Boca, el vecindario italiano que tiene casas de muchos colores.

Con cariño,
Damián

6 According to the postcard, Damián is living
F in a boarding house.
G near a café.
H from a pension.
J with some Spaniards.

7 Like similar national structures, the Casa Rosada was probably named for its
A first inhabitant.
B its landscaping.
C interior color.
D exterior color.

8 Damián was probably disappointed at the Café Tortoni because he didn't
F dance the tango.
G see a celebrity.
H become famous.
J feel very good.

9 In the context of the postcard, the word **llama** probably refers to a(n)
A animal.
B desert.
C flame.
D dessert.

10 Tomorrow Damián hopes to visit
F a museum.
G a river.
H a neighborhood.
J a cathedral.

C Read the ad from a local newspaper. Then choose the best answer for each statement that follows.

Desde la última vez que te vi...

He escalado los picos andinos en Bolivia.
He bajado por los cráteres ecuatorianos.
He explorado la selva amazónica en Perú.
He buceado en el Pacífico y el Atlántico nicaragüenses.
He hecho senderismo en el desierto argentino.
He saltado en paracaídas en los cielos de Costa Rica.
He estado cerca de unos volcanes que echaban lava sobre México.
Me he relajado en las aguas termales en Chile.
He bailado el tango con unos porteños.

Pero nunca he conocido nada ni a nadie como tú.
¿Todavía somos amigos?

¿Quieres mandarle un mensaje especial a alguien?
Tenemos tarjetas que lo dicen todo.

Papelería Andrade, Calle Mendoza 27, Buenos Aires
Tel: 290 7963

---

11 In the context of the ad, the word **escalado** probably refers to
 A diving.
 B hiking.
 C climbing.
 D jumping.

12 The narrator experienced the crater by
 F flying over it.
 G using binoculars.
 H climbing it.
 J going inside it.

13 The narrator saw the desert by
 A hiking it.
 B joining a safari.
 C using a map.
 D photographing it.

14 The narrator completed one of his or her activities with
 F Costa Ricans.
 G Argentines.
 H Chileans.
 J Peruvians.

15 This ad is probably directed to the person who wants to express
 A dislike.
 B anger.
 C happiness.
 D affection.

Complete the following tasks in writing.

16 Imagine that a friend is going to study in Buenos Aires and that he or she has written to ask you some questions about what to see and how to pay for things. Write an e-mail in Spanish to the friend telling him or her about interesting places to visit and how to pay for various products and services.

17 Imagine that you are studying in Buenos Aires for a year and that a friend wants to visit you in December. Write a postcard in English describing three or four things you can do or see there at that time of year. Use some of the information you learned about Buenos Aires in this chapter.

18 Imagine that you are in a tourism office in Buenos Aires and that you want some information about the city. Write a conversation in Spanish that includes your questions about sites, hours, and fees, and the responses of the tourism worker.

MATH TEST 2   **CAPÍTULO 10**

Imagine that you have a summer job in a bank and that you are called on to deal with foreign as well as U.S. currency. Calculate the amount your customers receive when they exchange one national currency for another. Round to the nearest whole number.

Cambio de moneda

Moneda *(currency)*	divisa *(foreign currency)*
1 US dólar	0.79 euro
1 euro	1.25 US dólares
1 US dólar	8 bolívares bolivianos
1 US dólar	431.6 colones costarricenses
1 nuevo sol peruano	4.6 córdobas nicaragüenses
1 US dólar	11.19 pesos mexicanos

1 ¿Cuántos euros recibe el cliente por 57 dólares US?

  A 42

  B 43

  C 44

  D 45

2 ¿Cuántos pesos mexicanos recibe por 360 dólares US?

  F 4,010

  G 4,028

  H 4,030

  J 4,040

3 ¿Cuántas córdobas nicaragüenses recibe por 32 nuevos soles peruanos?

  A 132

  B 137

  C 142

  D 147

4 ¿Cuántos bolívares bolivianos recibe por 42 dólares US?

  F 336

  G 342

  H 345

  J 348

5 ¿Cuántos colones costarricenses recibe por 25 dólares US?

  A 10,770

  B 10,790

  C 10,810

  D 10,830

MATH TEST 2   **CAPÍTULO 10**

Read each question and choose the best answer. Then mark the letter for the answer you have chosen.

6 Aproximadamente, la distancia promedio *(average)* entre la Tierra y la Luna es de 384,000 kilómetros. ¿Cómo se expresa esta distancia en la notación científica?

   F 3.84×10^{-5} km

   G 3.84×10^{-4} km

   H 3.84×10^{4} km

   J 3.84×10^{5} km

7 Si $9x - 12 = 42$, entonces $6x =$ _____

   A 12

   B 18

   C 24

   D 36

8 Teresa recibió una nota *(grade)* promedio de 86 en 5 exámenes. Después de los primeros cuatro exámenes, tuvo una nota promedio de 84. ¿Qué nota recibió en el quinto examen?

   F 88

   G 91

   H 94

   J 99

9 El área de un cuadrado *(square)* es de 64 centímetros cuadrados. ¿Cuál es el perímetro del cuadrado?

   A 16

   B 24

   C 32

   D 40

10 El diámetro de un círculo es de 12 cm. ¿Cuál es la circunferencia?

   F 12π cm

   G 18π cm

   H 24π cm

   J 36π cm

Holt Spanish 2

Score Sheets and Answers

Spanish 2 ¡Exprésate!

Standardized Assessment Tutor

Reading

1 Ⓐ Ⓑ Ⓒ Ⓓ   6 Ⓕ Ⓖ Ⓗ Ⓙ   11 Ⓐ Ⓑ Ⓒ Ⓓ

2 Ⓕ Ⓖ Ⓗ Ⓙ   7 Ⓐ Ⓑ Ⓒ Ⓓ   12 Ⓕ Ⓖ Ⓗ Ⓙ

3 Ⓐ Ⓑ Ⓒ Ⓓ   8 Ⓕ Ⓖ Ⓗ Ⓙ   13 Ⓐ Ⓑ Ⓒ Ⓓ

4 Ⓕ Ⓖ Ⓗ Ⓙ   9 Ⓐ Ⓑ Ⓒ Ⓓ   14 Ⓕ Ⓖ Ⓗ Ⓙ

5 Ⓐ Ⓑ Ⓒ Ⓓ   10 Ⓕ Ⓖ Ⓗ Ⓙ   15 Ⓐ Ⓑ Ⓒ Ⓓ

Writing

16 _____

_____

_____

_____

_____

_____

_____

_____

_____

_____

_____

17 _____

_____

_____

_____

_____

_____

_____

_____

_____

_____

_____

Nombre _____ Clase _____ Fecha _____

18 _____

_____

_____

_____

_____

_____

_____

_____

_____

_____

_____

Math

1 Ⓐ Ⓑ Ⓒ Ⓓ   5 Ⓐ Ⓑ Ⓒ Ⓓ   9 Ⓐ Ⓑ Ⓒ Ⓓ

2 Ⓕ Ⓖ Ⓗ Ⓙ   6 Ⓕ Ⓖ Ⓗ Ⓙ   10 Ⓕ Ⓖ Ⓗ Ⓙ

3 Ⓐ Ⓑ Ⓒ Ⓓ   7 Ⓐ Ⓑ Ⓒ Ⓓ

4 Ⓕ Ⓖ Ⓗ Ⓙ   8 Ⓕ Ⓖ Ⓗ Ⓙ

CAPÍTULO 1

1 C 2 G 3 C 4 F 5 D 6 J 7 A 8 F
9 D 10 H 11 A 12 J 13 C 14 G 15 B

16 Answers will vary. Example:

¿Qué tal, Natalia? Estoy en la Ciudad de México con mis tíos y mis primas. Los padres son simpáticos y serios. Sus dos hijas tienen diecinueve y veinte años y son simpáticas y extrovertidas. A ellas les gusta salir al cine, pero yo prefiero jugar al béisbol. Les encanta leer novelas y tienen casi tantos libros como mis tres hermanos. Estoy leyendo uno ahora. Tu amigo, Paco

17 Answers will vary. Example:

Dear Parents:

Since I've been to Mexico City, Ms. Durán has asked me to write you about a class trip there. We'll learn how the city was built on top of the old Aztec capital Tenochtitlán. We'll see art by Rivera and Kahlo and go to the floating gardens of Xochimilco. We'll also go to a **quinceañera** to celebrate a girl's special fifteenth birthday. We'll speak Spanish and write travel diaries in Spanish. Please call Lidia Durán for details at 435-9805. Ramón Baeza

18 Answers will vary. Example:

Pilar: Bienvenida a Brookton, Evita. ¿Qué tal? ¿Qué te gusta de la vída aquí?

Evita: Gracias. Esta escuela es más grande que mi otra escuela, pero los estudiantes son tan simpáticos como los otros. También me parece que hay menos que hacer aquí, no hay museos y plazas, como en la Ciudad de México. Estudio mucho y nunca salgo.

Pilar: Bueno, son tus primeros días aquí. ¡Ven al cine esta noche con nosotros!

CAPÍTULO 2

1 C 2 F 3 D 4 J 5 B 6 H 7 D 8 G
9 B 10 F 11 D 12 F 13 A 14 H 15 B

16 Answers will vary. Example:

Juan me escribió la semana pasada. Necesita pensar en su futuro. A él le encanta jugar al fútbol. También le gusta ayudar a sus hermanos menores cuando quieren aprender a nadar y montar en bicicleta. Sus padres son argentinos y Juan habla español con frecuencia. Le digo que debe ir a la universidad. Después puede ser profesor de español y entrenador en un colegio. ¿Qué le dices tú?

17 Answers will vary. Example:

Dear Mom and Dad,

I'd like to go with my Spanish class to Cuzco, Peru, in June. We'll learn how the Spanish colonized the capital of the Incan Empire and we'll attend Inti Raymi, the sun festival, to celebrate the Incan New Year. I'd also like to hear **quechua,** the Incan language. I hope to be a Spanish teacher one day, so I need to experience the culture and practice my Spanish. I hope you'll let me go! Love you! María Elena

18 Answers will vary. Example:

Sra. López: ¿Qué tal tu viaje a Perú?

Carlos: Muy bien. Viví con una familia en Cuzco, pasé horas en la casa y fui a muchos lugares interesantes.

Sra. López: ¿Qué viste en Cuzco?

Carlos: Vi una iglesia, una plaza y unas paredes antiguas. Me encantó ver las cosas incaicas.

Sra. López: ¿Usaste el español que aprendiste en esta clase?

Carlos: ¡Sí, señora, lo usé cuando fui al mercado!

CAPÍTULO 3

1 D **2** F **3** C **4** G **5** B **6** F **7** D **8** H
9 B **10** J **11** B **12** J **13** A **14** F **15** B

16 Answers will vary. Example:

Tengo que hacer unas diligencias hoy. Primero, quiero ir al centro recreativo a hacer gimnasia. Segundo, voy a ir a la peluquería a cortarme el pelo. Tercero, necesito comprar un billete en la estación para el sábado. Cuarto, necesito conseguir una licencia de conducir, pero no sé adónde ir. Voy a preguntare a alguien. Ahora, ¡necesito buscar la parada del metro!

17 Answers will vary. Example:

Hi, Jeremy! I'm glad you're coming to visit me in the capital city! It was founded in 1496 by Bartolomé Colón, Cristóbal's brother, so we'll see monuments and buildings related to that family. The Alcázar de Colón is an impressive fortress, and the Faro a Colón is a cross-shaped lighthouse. We'll also go to Boca Chica Beach, and we'll eat **locrio,** a Dominican dish with seafood, chicken, pork, or beef. See you soon! Alejo.

18 Answers will vary. Example:

Olivia: Perdóneme, ¿me podría decir dónde está la Calle Luz?

Sra. Alas: Sí, claro. ¿Qué número?

Olivia: Es el 347, el Salón «Josefa y José».

Sra. Alas: Bueno, hay que ir en metro. De aquí, siga derecho una cuadra hasta la Calle Flores, donde está la parada «Enriquillo». El tren para en la Calle Luz. Súbase a la calle, siga una cuadra y va a estar en el salón.

Olivia: Muchas gracias, señora.

CAPÍTULO 4

1 D **2** F **3** A **4** G **5** A **6** H **7** C **8** F
9 A **10** G **11** A **12** J **13** B **14** G **15** C

16 Answers will vary. Example:

¡Hola, Samuel! Bueno, ayer fue la competencia de debate y me dio tristeza. Perdimos. No ganamos nada y fue todo un fracaso. Me dio vergüenza. Cuando ganó el otro equipo, se pusieron a gritar y a reírse, pero nosotros reaccionamos mal. Nos fuimos al hotel, donde algunos se pusieron a llorar. Esto me dio ganas de no estar más en estas competencias, pero me gusta el debate y voy a seguir participando en el equipo. ¿Qué tal estuvo la competencia de bandas? Tu amigo, Jacobo.

17 Answers will vary. Example:

Hi, Ana, and greetings from Miami! Yesterday, I went to the famous Calle Ocho Festival in Little Havana, ate great Cuban food, and saw fireworks. Then, I saw a Cuban play in the Teatro de Bellas Artes. Tomorrow I'm going water skiing and then I'm going to see a jai alai match. I'd like to come back here in May for the CubaNostalgia Festival. See you soon! Penélope.

18 Answers will vary. Example:

Dra. Luna: ¿Qué te pasó, Arantxa?

Arantxa: Me caí en en el Parque del Dominó. Me di un golpe en el codo y me torcí el tobillo. Me duelen mucho. ¿Qué debo hacer?

Dra. Luna: Bueno, no te rompiste el codo y tienes el tobillo hinchado pero no roto. Tómate dos aspirinas cada tres horas y descansa por dos o tres días. Cuídate mucho.

Arantxa: Sí, doctora Luna, y gracias.

CAPÍTULO 5

1 C 2 G 3 B 4 F 5 B 6 F 7 C 8 J
9 A 10 H 11 C 12 G 13 A 14 F 15 C

16 Answers will vary. Example:

¡Hola, Abuelo!

Hoy conocí a un nuevo estudiante que se llama Julio. Conversamos un poco sobre nuestro interés en trotar. ¡Hace cinco años que trota Julio y cinco años que troto yo! Intercambiamos números de teléfono y él me recoge el sábado para ir a trotar. El próximo sábado, Julio y yo vamos al parque a trotar. A él y amí nos gusta jugar a fútbol también, Vamos a jugar al fútbol después de trotar. ¡Te quiero mucho, y no tardes en responder a esta nota! Pablo.

17 Dear Máximo, I'm in San José visiting my friend Leo. Yesterday we toured the city. We went to the Edificio Metálico, a building made entirely of metal, and to the Museo de Oro, which has a large collection of pre-Columbian gold ornaments. We also went to the Avenida Central to a restaurant and to the big pedestrian zone. See you soon! Estrella.

18 Answers will vary. Example:

Lola: Mamá, almuerzo ahora.

Mamá: Claro, pero necesito saber si todo estuvo bien esta mañana. ¿Te acordaste de cerrar la puerta?

Lola: Sí, la cerré con llave.

Mamá: ¿Llevaste el paraguas y el impermeable?

Lola: ¡Me olvidé de llevarlos por completo!

Mamá: Tranquila, hija. Te recogemos si es necesario. No te preocupes.

Lola: Gracias, mamá. Nos vemos.

Math Test 1

1 C 2 G 3 C 4 F 5 B 6 F 7 C 8 H
9 D 10 H

CAPÍTULO 6

1 B 2 J 3 D 4 H 5 A 6 H 7 A 8 J
9 D 10 G 11 A 12 J 13 B 14 H 15 C

16 Answers will vary. Example:

Querido diario, Hoy fue el día del nacimiento de mi hermano Felipe. Yo estaba en la clase de español cuando mi profesora me dijo que mi tío Miguel estaba en el colegio. Cuando lo vi me sentí muy contenta porque él también estaba muy contento. Me dijo que Felipe llegó a las once de la mañana. Cuando supe que tenía un hermano, ¡me puse a llorar de alegría!

Catalina

17 Answers will vary. Example:

Hi, Isabel! I really like Segovia. It's pretty as well as historic, with the snowy peaks of the Sierra de Guadarrama above and the Clamor and Eresma rivers below. The houses are old and have small windows and thick stone walls to keep out the heat. You'd love the palaces here, especially the Alcázar. See you soon! Tomás.

18 Answers will vary. Example:

Alba: Buenos días, señora. ¿Me puede decir cómo se llega a los teléfonos?

Señora Linares: Sí, está a cinco cuadras de aquí, a la derecha y al otro lado de la carretera. ¿Por qué no haces la llamada con tu teléfono?

Alba: Mi teléfono está roto y quiero llamar a mi familia.

Señora Linares: Puedes hacer la llamada allí.

Alba: Gracias por su ayuda.

CAPÍTULO 7

1 C 2 G 3 B 4 G 5 A 6 H 7 A 8 G
9 D 10 J 11 A 12 H 13 C 14 G 15 D

16 Answers will vary. Example:

Vamos a almorzar sándwiches, una ensalada y postre. Vamos a tomar té con un poquito de azúcar. Preparo los sándwiches con pan tostado, pollo horneado y mostaza dulce. Para la ensalada de lechuga, tomates y huevos picados, añadimos aceite y vinagre al gusto. De postre sirvo fresas y plátanos frescos y los sirvo con una salsa de chocolate derretido. Creo que todo va a estar muy sabroso.

17 Answers will vary. Example:

Hi, Tomás! I'm enjoying San Juan. I like the cultural diversity of Puerto Rico, where many people have African, Spanish, or Taino roots. I've visited the Iglesia de San José, which was built in 1532 in Spanish Gothic style, and the Casa Blanca, built in 1521 for the Ponce de León family. It's now a museum. You should see the Parque de las Palomas, which has great views of the bay. Later! Vicente.

18 Answers will vary. Example:

Genaro: ¿Me ayudas a comer mejor?

Natalia: ¿Qué desayunas?

Genaro: Nada. Duermo tarde.

Natalia: Toma cereal y un vaso de jugo para la energía. ¿Qué almuerzas?

Genaro: Una hamburguesa y unas papas fritas.

Natalia: Bueno, las proteínas son importantes, pero necesitas evitar la sal y la comida frita. ¿Que cenas?

Genaro: Helado o pastel.

Natalia: Come frutas, vegetales y carne. ¡Cuídate, amigo mío!

CAPÍTULO 8

1 D 2 F 3 A 4 H 5 C 6 J 7 B 8 J
9 C 10 F 11 C 12 H 13 A 14 G 15 B

16 Answers will vary. Example:

¡Hola, Luz! Fui de compras hoy en una tienda del barrio París-Londres. Buscaba adornos para mi cuarto y encontré los más bonitos del mundo. Compré una cesta de paja para mis cadenas y collares. Luego compré una pintura de los Andes y una manta tejida para mi habitación. Los primeros dos artículos estaban en liquidación y me costaron poco. Tuve que regatear para el tercero, que valía $70, y me lo dejaron en $53. Un abrazo, Delia.

17 Answers will vary. Example:

Dear Mr. Rodríguez, I'm in Santiago, and I thought of your class today when I learned about two men who are important in Chilean history. First, I visited a plaza named for Bernardo O'Higgins, who helped to liberate the country in 1818. Then, I saw La Chascona, one of three houses the poet Pablo Neruda designed and lived in. It's a creative place with lots of glass and gardens. See you! Teodoro.

18 Answers will vary. Example:

Miguel: ¿En qué le puedo servir, señor?

Señor Ortiz: Busco una corbata roja.

Miguel: Tenemos una corbata de lana y una de seda. ¿Cuál prefiere?

Señor Ortiz: Prefiero la de seda.

Miguel: Bueno. ¿Le gusta ésta?

Señor Ortiz: Sí, ¿cuánto vale?

Miguel: Vale $64.80 con el impuesto.

Señor Ortiz: Le doy mi tarjeta de crédito.

Miguel: Y le doy su corbata y su recibo. Gracias, señor.

CAPÍTULO 9

1 D **2** H **3** A **4** H **5** D **6** F **7** B **8** G
9 D **10** F **11** A **12** J **13** B **14** J **15** A

16 Answers will vary. Example:

¡Hola, Mario! Me dijiste que querías hacer camping en julio en el desierto de Arizona. Prefiero ir a las montañas de Colorado. Hará menos calor y estará menos seco allá que en el desierto. Si la temperatura es alta, encontraremos árboles. Habrá un lago cerca y podremos nadar y pescar. Creo que también veremos más animales y pájaros en las montañas. El desierto es árido y no hay nada. ¿Qué veremos, qué haremos en él? Me interesan más las montañas. Ernesto.

17 Answers will vary. Example:

Dear Susan, Yesterday I saw some interesting buildings here in El Paso. I went first to the Ysleta Mission, a building important to the native Tigua. Then I visited the University of Texas in El Paso. Its buildings were designed like those in Bhutan, a Himalayan country. I also saw the Magoffin House, which combines adobe with wooden decorations in the Victorian style. I learned a lot! Alejandro.

18 Answers will vary. Example:

Violeta: Mamá, ¿qué llevaré a la playa? Ya tengo mi traje de baño.

Mamá: ¿Van ustedes a bañarse todo el tiempo?

Violeta: Claro que no. Nos interesa observar la naturaleza, mirar pájaros, buscar caracoles, explorar cuevas tal vez...

Mamá: Parece que estarás afuera todo el tiempo. Lleva tus gafas de sol y la crema protectora. No te olvides de llevar tu tienda de campaña y tu linterna. ¡Y espero que te diviertas!

Violeta: Sí, mamá, y muchas gracias.

CAPÍTULO 10

1 B **2** J **3** A **4** G **5** D **6** F **7** D **8** G
9 C **10** H **11** C **12** J **13** A **14** G **15** D

16 Answers will vary. Example:

¡Hola, José! Fue un placer ayudarte. Y ahora: tendrás que usar pesos argentinos que conseguirás en un banco en tu pueblo o en Buenos Aires. En la ciudad, podrás darles dólares en efectivo, cheques de viajero o una tarjeta de crédito. No aceptarán un cheque de tu banco. Recomiendo que visites la Boca y La Casa Rosada. Espero que estés bien. Un saludo, Laura.

17 Answers will vary. Example:

Dear Nuria, You're coming here! Since December is summer, we'll go to the beach in Mar del Plata or in Punta del Este, Uruguay. We'll also ride the **colectivo,** a small bus that you have to hop on and off very quickly! We can shop, and Florida Street is the place to do it. And let's go to a concert. Maybe Daniel Barenboim will conduct. See you soon! Amanda.

18 Answers will vary. Example:

Señor Lugones: ¿En qué puedo servirle?

Adán: ¿Me podría dar información sobre Buenos Aires?

Señor Lugones: Le ofrezco este plano de la ciudad y una guía de atracciones.

Adán: Gracias. ¿Me podría decir cuándo se abren los museos mañana?

Señor Lugones: Están cerrados los lunes. Los martes están abiertos y son gratis.

Math Test 2

1 D **2** G **3** D **4** F **5** B **6** J **7** D **8** H
9 C **10** F